Dedication

This book is for my three incredible grandchildren, Matthew Dale, Alexis Meyers, and Norah Meyers. You help me see things through the eyes of a child. You help me appreciate the little things in life and make me want to continue sharing stories that need to be told.—**Lois Szymanski**

This book is dedicated to Elizabeth Spino, who taught me almost everything I know about the Chincoteague ponies, and to Captain Dan, whose wonderful pontoon boat rides enabled me to take many pony and scenery pictures that helped me illustrate this book.—**Linda Kantjas**

The Legendary Stallion of Chincoteague

SURFER DUDE

Lois Szymanski

Illustrated
by Linda Kantjas

Schiffer Publishing Ltd®
4880 Lower Valley Road • Atglen, PA 19310

Gremlin raised her head, inhaling salty ocean air and fresh spring grass. To this wild pony mare, the aroma was a bouquet of sweet promise. She lowered her head to graze. Warm weather had finally come to Assateague Island.

It is time, Gremlin thought. She followed her stallion, Pirate, and his other mares, her sisters. Gremlin watched Mappy prance ahead with her new foal. Soon the foal would have a friend.

It is time. The full silver moon whispered to Gremlin, chasing the sun from the sky. She lowered herself to the ground at the meadow's edge. Pirate nuzzled her and then turned to take the other mares to graze.

The colt slid into the world, warm and wet. Gremlin rubbed her velvety nose over his body. Something told her this one was special. He would carry on the legacy. Crowds would come to see him and love him.

The colt's ears drooped like a puppy dog, but as his blood circulated, they came up slowly. His momma rumbled messages of love from deep in her throat.

The colt's chocolatey chestnut coat and silver mane and tail matched those of his momma. A bright white diamond on his forehead became a starting point for the stripe that ran down his nose, widening at the bottom to drop between his nostrils and continue all the way to his lower lip.

When Gremlin licked the whorl on his forehead, she noticed something extra special about her new colt. He had a blue eye.

The colt scrambled to get up. He was anxious to know the world, but his legs would not cooperate. Every time he tried to stand, they tangled up. A few more tries, and then his spindly legs were all straightened out. Even though he was swaying, he was standing, and he liked that.

By morning, the colt had learned to trot. He scampered around the meadow, scooting under his momma's tail to hide and then dashing out again. And nose to nose, he met his first friend, Mappy's foal.

The colt was a few days old when he heard a whooping sound followed by the thunder of hooves. The colt shivered and followed his momma, darting to follow the herd, pushed on by men on horseback. Together, they trotted through tall grasses. They splashed through a creek and continued up an incline and into a large pen.

Inside the fence, the colt watched the cowboys push his momma through a chute. The spring roundup vet opened his momma's mouth and fed her worm medicine. She licked pasty white goop from her lips and came out of the chute. She nudged her son to move to the far side of the pen with Pirate and the rest of their band.

The colt looked around the pen at ponies he had only seen from a distance. There were many herds, each with a stallion leading his group of mares and foals.

People stood around the edges of the fence watching the ponies, taking photos, and shouting out gleefully.

One child climbed the fence and called to a man standing farther down the fence line.

"Daddy, daddy!" she yelled.

Her father walked over to stand beside her.

"I like that one," she said pointing at Gremlin's colt.

Her dad narrowed his eyes against the sun, then smiled. "You picked a good one, Jenny," he said. "The fire company is going to keep that one. He'll be a fine stallion one day and will father handsome foals that will be sold to raise money for the fire department."

"I think you should name him Surfer Dude," she said with a giggle.

Two saltwater cowboys had joined them at the fence.

"I think that is a fine name," one of them said, chuckling. The other one nodded.

And just like that, Surfer Dude got his name.

After a veterinarian checked them, the herds were released. Surfer Dude stuck close to his momma. They followed Pirate down trails covered with pine needles and through muddy marshes.

The summer stretched out, long and hot with buzzing flies and mosquitoes. Some days the herd stood on the edge of the bay, facing Chincoteague Island. Surfer Dude watched boats zipping past, people clamming on the point, and people near the houses across the water on Chincoteague. Sometimes the horses stood beneath the shade of the tall, red-and-white striped Assateague lighthouse.

When the mosquitoes became too pesky, the herd waded into the ocean on the other side of the island, turning their backs to the surf so waves could wash away the clinging insects.

Another foal soon joined the herd. Surfer and his two young friends ran along the beach, bucking and dodging the waves. Life was good.

In late summer, the cowboys came again. They drove Pirate and his herd into the south pen with other bands of ponies. The next day, more ponies came—ponies Surfer Dude had never seen, from the far north end of the island.

People came to visit the ponies and take photos. The vet checked each pony. Cowboys wandered around inside the pens. Someone slapped a tag on Surfer Dude's rump and a red string around his neck.

Gremlin rubbed her son's nose. She knew that string meant he would be staying.

When the cowboys opened the gates the next morning, the ponies were not turned out. The cowboys herded them forward to a point of land. There they stood, looking out over the bay. After a while, the sound of a horn cut the quiet morning air. A plume of orange smoke filled the sky as the cowboys drove the herd forward into the water.

Surfer Dude paddled his legs when the land disappeared under his hooves. His eyes rolled with fear. He felt his momma paddling alongside and realized he was okay. He could swim! In no time at all, they were scrambling ashore. Hundreds of people were cheering for them. Surfer Dude liked that!

The ponies trotted down the streets of Chincoteague. On both sides of the road people cheered them on. Surfer followed his momma, trotting into the pen at the back of the carnival grounds.

There was an auction the next day and many of the foals were sold, but Surfer Dude stayed at his momma's side. He watched as his friends were separated into another pen. They

would go to new homes. Only a few, like Surfer Dude, would stay on the island.

On Friday, the day after the auction, the herds swam home.

As summer turned to fall and then winter, Surfer Dude grew tall and fuzzy. Snow and ice came swirling down, making an icy crust that coated the island. Surfer learned to paw the snow and ice away to find salty cordgrass underneath. He learned to chew bark from trees and which bushes and berries he could eat.

The herd moved into the warm pine forests on cold days and out to the beach when spring brought warm winds.

As the years passed, Surfer became accustomed to the roundups. He liked the way a cowboy sometimes scratched his itchy back. One day, he followed two cowboys down the fence line, watching them hammer new wire to posts.

One cowboy stopped hammering and stared at the yearling colt.

"He sure is a handsome dude," he said.

The second cowboy stopped to look. "Yes, he is. I'm glad we kept him," he replied.

Just after Surfer Dude turned two, Pirate drove the colt from the herd, biting and pushing the foal away. Surfer Dude was confused. He wanted his momma!

The thick colt stood and watched his herd. He snorted and paced. And when the stallion looked away, Surfer Dude tried to enter the circle again. These mares were his family—the only family he had ever known. But Pirate rolled his eyes and charged the colt again, teeth bared.

Finally, Surfer lowered his head and wandered away. His father was telling him, "Son, it is time to grow up. Go find a herd of your own."

Surfer wandered alone for a few days before he met up with two other young colts. The three formed a band of boys and stuck together for several seasons.

At his fourth spring roundup, Surfer Dude set his eyes on a pretty little chestnut filly. His heart hammered. He knew the time had come to have a herd of his own.

When summer roundup rolled around, Surfer Dude gained another mare—a bay and white pinto. And on his fifth birthday he brought in a third mare. Over the years his herd would grow and grow, but the pretty chestnut mare the cowboys called Surf Queen was always his favorite girl.

Surfer Dude's silver mane grew thick and long. His forelock fell over his eyes in sparkling strands. His thick, muscular body rippled in the sunlight. He was not only a handsome and strong stallion, he was also kind and gentle.

Each year Surfer Dude's herd grew with new foals that he nurtured and loved. And each year those foals brought a high price at auction. Out in the wild, caring for his herd, Surfer Dude could not know how the people loved him, how they sought him out, how everyone wanted a photo of "that handsome stallion named Surfer Dude on the south end of Assateague Island." People gathered at the fence at every roundup, looking for him.

"Look at those beautiful eyes," someone would say. "One eye is blue and the other one has a blue line around it."

"That's Surfer Dude," another person would reply. He only tossed his head and watched them, loving the soft sound of their voices.

When he was seventeen years old, Surfer Dude's pretty chestnut mare, Surf Queen, had a tiny foal with a chocolatey colored coat and a silver mane. Except for the fact that the colt had more white on his nose than Surfer Dude, he was the image of his father.

At the pony penning roundup, the firemen said they were not keeping any colts. They would all be sold.

"We have too many boys on the island," one fireman said. "We're only keeping fillies."

But as one person after another came forward to share how much they loved the colt, the firemen changed their minds. On the day of the auction, fireman Roe Terry stepped up to the microphone.

"Surfer Dude is getting older," Roe said. "His foals have sold for top dollar year after year. This colt looks just like him, so we've decided to keep him, to carry on the legacy."

The crowd cheered and the bidding started. The highest bidder, who was granted the right to name the colt, dubbed him Surfer Dude's Riptide.

Riptide grew tall and handsome, a replica of his father. For some reason, Surfer Dude allowed him to stay in the herd much longer than usual.

"I can't believe Riptide is still in Surfer's herd," one woman said at roundup. "Why hasn't he driven the colt away?"

"His father knows he is special," her friend replied. "He's grooming him to take over the herd one day."

"Maybe you are right," the first woman replied.

Finally, when Riptide was three years old, Surfer chased his son from the herd. The cowboys sent Riptide north where he was separated from his old herd by two fences, but he escaped, wandering between the fences for some time.

Soon Riptide joined up with another young colt named Chief. The two colts became fast friends, sticking together even after they were both moved north again.

Mother Nature whispered on the breeze, sending a message to Riptide and Chief. *It is time. Time to grow up. Time to find a herd of your own.* And so the two friends separated, going off to find mares of their own.

Riptide settled into herd life with his three mares, Skylark, Sweetheart, and Lady Hook. Just down the service road on the south end of the island, his father heard Mother Nature whispering, but this time the message was different. Surfer Dude knew his end was drawing near.

Now twenty-three years old, the stallion was losing weight and was ready to leave for greener pastures in the world beyond. Spring was almost upon them. Birds were making nests in the trees, but winter had settled in Surfer Dude's bones. He nudged his mares. *It is time,* his nudging said. *It is time to bring my son.*

His mares understood. Only Surf Queen remained at his side as the others pushed through the fence and trotted down the service road toward the north end of Assateague Island.

Within days, the mares were back. They had enticed Riptide to leave his mares and come home to the south end of the island.

Surfer Dude saw his son coming. They touched noses. Surfer moved to the edge of his herd as Riptide came in.

Both stallions knew that two boys could not share one herd, but they respected each other. There would be no dramatic battle on hind legs. There would be no gnashing of teeth or hooves striking hide. Yet there would be a dance between them as Surfer prepared to say goodbye.

For several weeks the father and the son took turns being in charge of the herd. Some days, Riptide would be in the center of the mares with his father on the outside looking in. Other days, Surfer Dude stood among his ladies, touching their noses, whuffing softly, saying goodbye.

One morning, the sun rose round and hot in the sky and the air felt to Surfer Dude just like the morning he was born. The sun warmed his back as he turned it toward the herd.

It is time, Mother Nature whispered in his ear. *Another world is waiting.*

Surfer heard the sound of hooves thundering above. When he looked up, there was his father, Pirate, taking shape in the clouds, with Gremlin at his side. The wind blew and the clouds separated. A longing filled the twenty-three-year-old stallion. He was tired and weak and needed his momma, and there she was, right on the other side.

He gazed at his herd. Surf Queen stared back, longing in her eyes. She raised her nose and nickered. Surfer Dude shook his head, the heavy mane tickling his neck. Riptide was now in the center of his herd. They would be safe in his care.

It is time. The words rose from the rippling grasses. They whistled through the branches and leaves of nearby trees.
It is time.

Surfer Dude walked away, into the trees, plodding at first. As he moved, excitement grew in his heart. He broke into a tired trot. Ahead, he could see Pirate and Gremlin, and, yes, there was Mappy, too. Others he had known galloped into the herd from the sides. There was Miracle Man, Virginia Belle, and North Star, too. Just ahead were stallions and mares he had known—horses who had left this world before him, and all of them were together.

A golden light enveloped Surfer Dude as the earth rose to meet the clouds and sun. Joy and warmth filled his bones as he became part of the herd, galloping through the clouds. He felt young again. And when he looked down he could see his beloved herd, grazing with his son, Riptide. Surfer Dude would always watch over them, for they were part of him, just as the wind and sky, sun and stars are part of this stallion that so many have loved.

Each year, when Pony Penning returns to the island during the last full week in July, hundreds of voices speak his name. *Surfer Dude!* Visitors remember this loving stallion and his kind heart. They speak of how he nuzzled his foals and respected his mares. As Riptide's foals race through the herd, a truth is evident: Surfer Dude lives on in the very blood of his descendants. His legacy is alive.

Afterword

While this story has been romanticized in many ways, the facts are true. Surfer Dude was named by the daughter of a saltwater cowboy, and he allowed his son, Riptide, to stay with the herd much longer than is usual. Riptide roamed with the pony, Chief Golden Eagle, during his years as a bachelor stallion.

In the winter of 2014-2015, many people noticed that Surfer Dude was rapidly declining. Around that time, his mares did something highly unusual. They broke out of the fenced enclosure and traveled down the service road to the north end of the island to fetch Riptide, who left his own mares behind to follow Surfer Dude's mares.

After the cowboys rounded up the renegades, Riptide was put into the southern pens. There, many witnessed a dance of sorts between Surfer Dude and Riptide. Some days Surfer Dude was with the herd. Other days, he stood on the outside looking in while his son reigned. No violent fights were witnessed. Then, one day Surfer was gone. His body was found on the island in March 2015.

While Riptide exhibits his sire's beauty, he has not exhibited the same gentle nature. Some say it will come with age and wisdom. Only time will tell. This author believes that Surfer Dude's spirit will always reside on the island, watching over the family he loves.

Can you find these Assateague creatures in the story?

American oystercatcher – Oystercatchers live in areas with sandy beaches, salt marshes, and tidal flats, where they feed on shellfish or marine worms. To open an oyster, mussel, or clam, they jab their bill into an opening, cut the muscles, and clean out the contents. Other times they hammer the shell until it breaks open, and then eat the contents.

Bald eagle – A symbol of the United States of America, the bald eagle is both a predator and a scavenger, sometimes sweeping up prey in its powerful talons, other times eating dead fish swept ashore or other carrion. Their nests, in tall trees, are built of sticks lined with leaves, needles, and finer materials. They often use their nests for many years, adding to them. The nests can become as large as a queen-size mattress.

Belted kingfisher – The kingfisher feeds on fish and is interesting to watch. It plummets head first into the water, capturing small fish near the surface with its bill.

Cattle egret – The cattle egret is often seen with grazing animals and on the backs of the wild ponies of Assateague Island, consuming the insects that are its primary diet.

Delmarva fox squirrel – This large silver squirrel was once endangered. Thanks in part to the Chincoteague Wildlife Refuge, it has made a comeback and was removed from the endangered list in November 2015. A ground squirrel, this species is seldom seen hopping from tree branch to tree branch and is more likely to be found feeding on nuts and berries on the ground.

Diamondback terrapin turtle – This is the only species of turtle that spends its life in brackish waters. It feeds on fish, snails, crabs mollusks, carrion, clams, and worms. Excess salt is excreted through a gland in its eye. It hibernates beneath muddy creek inlets during winter and is named for the diamond-shaped growth rings on its top shell.

Eastern cottontail – One of the most common rabbit species in North America, it is found in meadows and shrubby areas. Eastern cottontails are vegetarian and dine mostly at night on grasses and herbs, and in the winter on bark, twigs, and plant buds.

Great blue heron – The largest heron in North America, the great blue heron can stand four feet tall. It lives in marshes, swamps, shorelines, and tidal flats, and forages mostly for fish, stabbing its prey quickly with its beak.

Great egret – The great egret is often seen standing like a statue in bay and inlet waters, waiting for a fish, which is quickly stabbed with its beak and eaten.

Green heron – Often called the little green heron, this bird has a green iridescence on its back that looks dull blue. It eats mostly small fish, but also grasshoppers, small snakes, and snails. Sometimes this smart bird drops a small feather or twig on the water surface, using it as bait to draw fish into striking range.

Laughing gull – Wading, swimming, or plunging in flight, the laughing gull catches crustaceans, insects, snails, small fish, and even worms to survive. Most migrate south when cold weather comes.

Northern cardinal – Cardinals like to nest in dense bushes. They feed on seeds, insects, grasses, grains, flowers, buds, and berries. The male is bright red, while the female (shown) is mottled brown, tan, and yellow.

Quail – Quail feed on leaves, seeds, berries, bulbs, insects, and acorns or other small nuts or pods. They are found in most parts of the United States.

Red-winged blackbird – Known for their boldness, red-winged blackbirds forage mostly on insects and grains, but also berries and small fruits. Males have red shoulder patches hidden under their body feathers; the patches are visible when they sing.

Sika deer – Sika deer are actually elk and hop like a kangaroo. They were brought to this country from Japan many years ago. Smaller than most species, they weigh about ninety pounds and stand two and a half feet at their rump.

White-tailed deer – White-tailed deer eat fruit and green plants, aquatic vegetation, nuts, acorns, grains, and even bark, twigs, and buds. Males grow antlers in the spring and shed them in late winter. They can grow to three and a half feet at the shoulder and weigh up to 500 pounds.

Ponies of Assateague

Angel Wings – Born in 2008, Angel Wings lost her life as a six-year-old with a foal at her side when she fell ill after the 2014 fall roundup. Her filly, Pixie Dust, was bottle fed and cared for on the Chincoteague Pony Farm and is now a beautiful wild mare on Assateague.

Bay Girl – A bay mare, Bay Girl walks with a slight limp from an old injury to her left rear hoof or fetlock. Riptide inherited her after Surfer Dude's passing.

Cinnamon Blaze – This beautiful chestnut mare was born in 1999. She has a wide blaze that covers only her right nostril. She has a light, hard-to-read "99" brand on her left hip.

Courtney's Island Dove – This 2006 chestnut pinto mare shares part of her name with her sire, Courtney's Boy. She spent several years with Surfer Dude and his herd.

Got Milk – This bay pinto mare was named for a white marking that looks like milk running down her chin. She was with Surfer Dude for several years and became one of Riptide's mares after Surfer Dude's passing.

Miracle Man – Miracle Man was rescued from the Chincoteague Wildlife Refuge as an orphan foal in 1995 by the Chincoteague family of Donald Leonard. He left this world in spring 2013, but many of the island's foals still exhibit the speckled coat he passed on.

North Star – The chestnut pinto named North Star was one of the foals kept in 1996 and sired by the Arabian stallion, Premierre. He was a well-loved stallion until his passing in 2012.

Virginia Bell – This chestnut mare was part of Surfer Dude's herd for at least the last ten years of her life. She is dam to Surfer Dude's Gidget, a popular island mare. Virginia Bell died in the winter of 2011-2012.

Yankee Spirit – Known in Maryland as Spirit of Assateague, this stallion is thought to have jumped the fence from Maryland to Virginia many years ago in pursuit of a mare. He was taken back to Maryland, but promptly jumped the fence again, and was taken back. The third time he jumped the fence, the cowboys were told to keep him. They changed his name to Yankee Spirit and he lived out the rest of his days on the refuge, passing sometime in the winter of 2014-2015.

Bibliography

The Chesapeake Bay Program. www.chesapeakebay.net/fieldguide.

National Audubon Society Field Guide to North American Birds. http://www.audubon.org/field-guide.

National Geographic. http://animals.nationalgeographic.com.

Wildlife Treks with Friends of the Chincoteague Wildlife Refuge. When visiting the Chincoteague National Wildlife Refuge, you can join in a Wildlife Trek by bus. Call the refuge's Herbert H. Bateman Educational and Administrative Center at 757-336-3696 for tickets. The center is at 8231 Beach Road, Chicoteague, Virginia 23336.

Library of Congress Control Number: 2017933326

Type set in Angsana New &Adine Kirnberg

ISBN: 978-0-7643-5366-6

Printed in China

Published by Schiffer Publishing, Ltd.
4880 Lower Valley Road
Atglen, PA 19310
Phone: (610) 593-1777; Fax: (610) 593-2002
E-mail: Info@schifferbooks.com
Web: www.schifferbooks.com